100 more cross-stitch luvable pets

Whether you're a cat person or dog person—fish, turtle, bird, mouse, bunny, or frog person—there's something for every pet lover in this inspiring collection of cross-stitch designs. Expanding upon the pets published in her first book of *99 Cross-stitch Luvable Pets*, Linda Gillum again captures some of the unique characteristics that make our pets special as they bring love, laughter, and companionship into our lives. The adorable motifs are perfect for stitching onto shirts, bags, pillows, hand towels, wall hangings, and more. Use them also to stitch special heirloom ornaments for yourself, family, and friends.

About the Artist

Linda Gillum, an award-winning needlework designer, is well known for her fabulous animal artwork. She had authored numerous cross-stitch and painting books and is a fine artist accomplished in oil pastels, as well as watercolor, acrylic, and oil painting. An avid animal lover, Linda is "mom" to two dogs and two cats and has enjoyed sharing her life with a host of other pets. Her humoristic approach and expert color skills have made her a popular designer with cross-stitchers throughout the world.

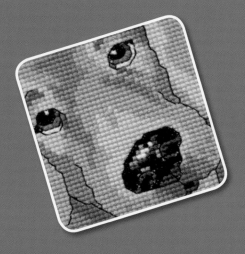

Contents

Dogs 5

Cats 33

Other Luvable Pets 46

MALTESE

CAVALIER KING
CHARLES SPANIEL

SHIH TZU

SPOILED ROTTEN
CATS LIVE HERE

SCHIPPERKE

GREAT DANE

TRIGGERFISH

WIRE-HAIRED FOX TERRIER

SIBERIAN HUSKY

BLOODHOUND

BURMESE

DOBERMAN

hi
mom

If you want the best
seat in the house...
move the dog

ENGLISH SETTER

BERNESE MOUNTAIN DOG

AIRDALE TERRIER

WELSH CORGI

AFGHAN HOUND

dogs believe
they are
human...
cats believe
they are
God.

COLLIE

BALINESE

BEST FRIENDS

there are cat people...

...and everybody else...

BeTTa

DANDIE DINMONT TERRIER

BRITISH SHORT HAIR

EXOTIC LONGHAIR

Cat's MoTTo:
No matter what
you've done wrong,
always make it look
like the dog
did it.

ENGLISH SPRINGER
SPANIEL

kittens kittens

kittens

JACK RUSSELL TERRIER

SHAR-PEI

welcome

Charts are in numerical order starting on page 5.

Back Cover

Front Cover

Page 2

Page 3

4

Baby Yorkie

size: 40 x 50

DMC	X	¼	BS
White	☆		
151	n	n	
152	✛		
301	⬆	⬆	
310	◼	◼	⬛
318	I	I	
402	L	L	
413	◆	◆	
702	⊥	⊥	
907	@	@	
951	Z	Z	
3721	♥	♥	⬛
3776	A	A	
3856	◔	◔	

LHASA APSO

Lhasa Apso

size: 38 x 28

DMC	X	¼	BS
White	☆	☆	
301	◆	◆	
310	◼	◼	⬛
402	m	m	
413	⬛	◪	⬛
414		⬆	
415	Z	Z	
792			⬛
951	❯	❯	
3776	▣	▣	⬛
3856	H	H	

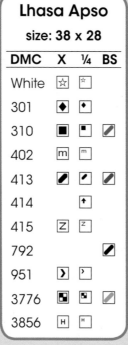

5

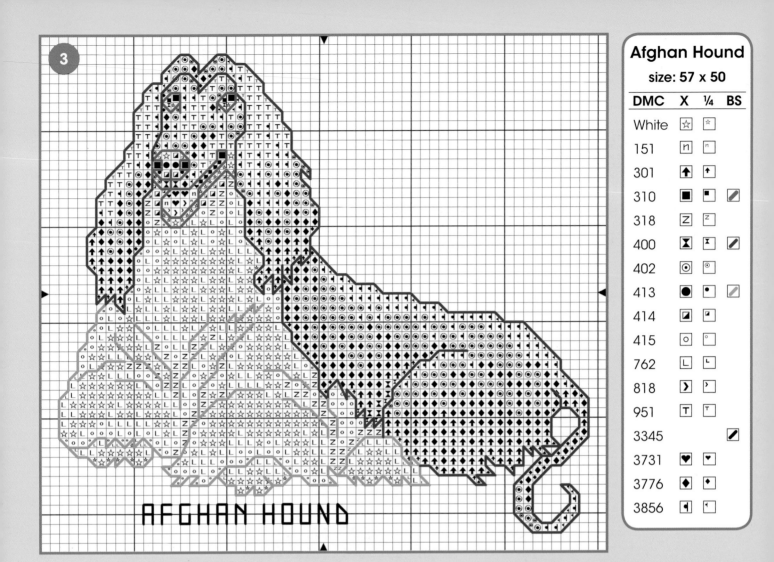

Afghan Hound

size: 57 x 50

DMC	X	¼	BS
White	☆	☆	
151	n	n	
301	↑	↑	
310	■	■	⁄
318	Z	z	
400	✕	✕	⁄
402	⊙	⊙	
413	●	●	⁄
414	◨	◨	
415	o	o	
762	L	L	
818	⟩	⟩	
951	T	T	
3345			⁄
3731	♥	♥	
3776	◆	◆	
3856	◀	◁	

AFGHAN HOUND

Baby Cocker

size: 52 x 34

DMC	X	¼	BS
White	☆		
151	Z	z	
223	⊞	⊞	
301	↑	↑	
310	■	■	⁄
350	✕	✕	
402		T	
414	◆	◆	
434	⁄	⁄	
435	◣	◣	
436	✚	✚	
721	◓	◓	
738	H	H	
739	⟩	⟩	
816	♥	♥	

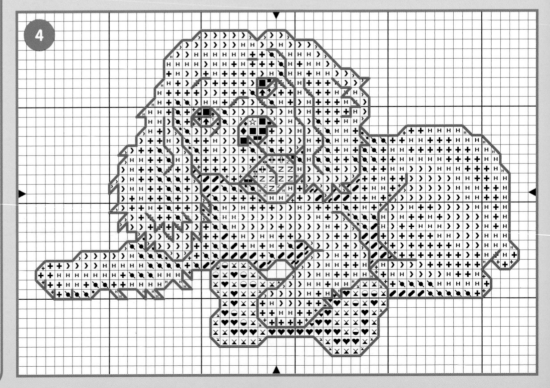

6

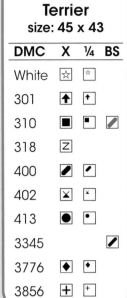

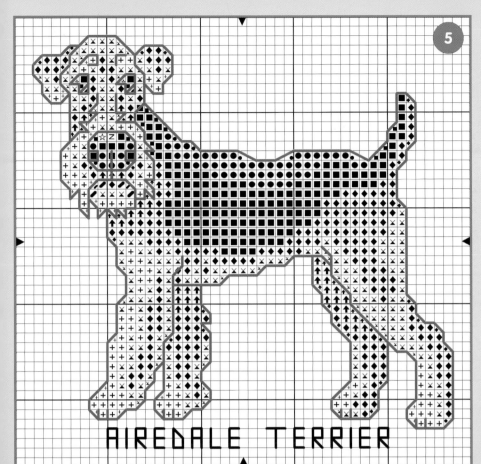

AIREDALE TERRIER

Airedale Terrier
size: 45 x 43

DMC	X	¼	BS
White	☆	☆	
301	⬆	⬆	
310	■	■	╱
318	Z		
400	╱	╱	
402	✕	ˣ	
413	●	●	
3345			╱
3776	◆	◆	
3856	➕	＋	

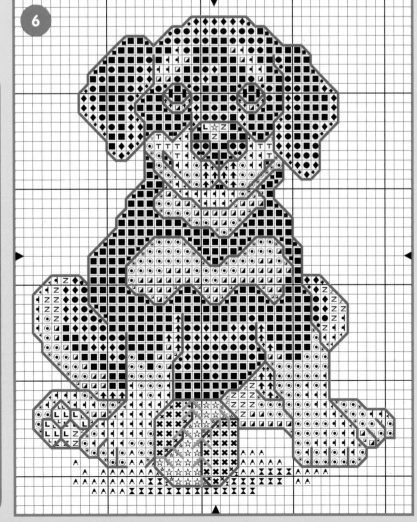

Baby Rottie
size: 39 x 50

DMC	X	¼	BS
White	☆	☆	╱
301	⬆	⬆	
310	■	■	╱
318	Z	ᶻ	
350			╱
402	⊙	⊙	
413	●	●	
414	◆	◆	
702	✕	✕	
762	L	ᴸ	
792	✖	✖	
907	◣	^	
951	T	ᵀ	
3776	◪	◪	
3856	◀	◀	

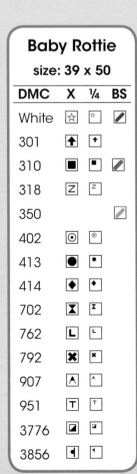

7

7

Baby Husky
size: 57 x 37

DMC	X	¼	BS	FK
White	☆	☆		
151	n	n		
310	■	▪	╱	•
318	Z	z		
350	✕	ˣ	╱	
402	◉	◉		
413	⬆	⬆		
762	I	I		
793	✕	ˣ		
809	m	m		
816	♥	♥		
839	◆	◆		
840	✕	✕		
841	◥	◥		
842	⊥	⊥		
950	‡	‡		
3747	○	○		
3770	❭	❭		
3776	❶	❶		

Baby Pom
size: 47 x 25

DMC	X	¼	BS
151	n	n	
301	⬆		
310	■	▪	╱
350	✕	ˣ	
402	◉	◉	
721	♠	•	
816	♥	♥	╱
951	T	T	
3776	✕	✕	
3856	★	★	

8

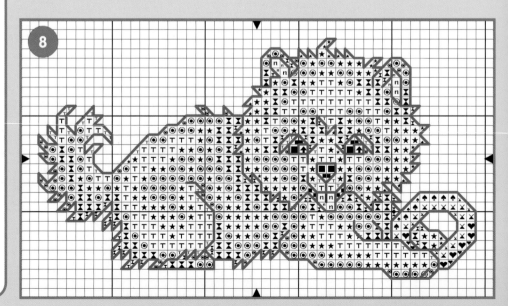

Bernese Mountain Dog
size: 39 x 41

DMC	X	¼	BS
White	☆	☆	
151	n	n	
301	◢	◢	
310	■	■	◿
318	✛	✛	
402	▲	^	
413	⬆	⬆	
414	✖	✖	◿
415	◣		
762	Z	z	
816	♥	♥	
3345			◿
3731	◀	◀	
3776	▲	▲	

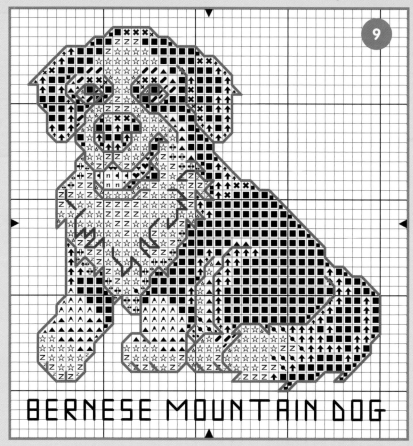

BERNESE MOUNTAIN DOG

Best Friend
size: 46 x 46

DMC	X	¼	BS
White	☆	☆	
151	n	n	
223	▲		
310	■	■	◿
318	✖	✖	
368	◀	◀	
413	⬆	⬆	
415	Z	z	
762	○	○	
818	I	I	
3345			◿
3721	♥	♥	

BEST FRIEND

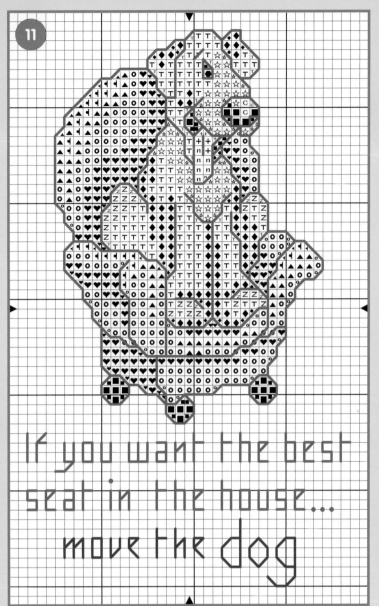

If you want the best
seat in the house...
move the dog

Best Seat

size: 35 x 58

DMC	X	¼	BS	FK
White	☆	☆		
151	n	n		
223	+	+		
310	■	■	◢	·
321	♥	♥	◢	
350	◉	◦		
400	⬢			
402	T	T		
414	C	C		
721	▲	▲		
722	◀	◀		
3776	◆	◆		
3856	Z	Z		

Border Collie

size: 29 x 38

DMC	X	¼	BS
White	☆	☆	
310	■	■	◢
318	✚	✚	
400		◆	
413	✖	✖	
414	◣	◣	
415	n	n	
762	T	T	
3345			◢

BORDER COLLIE

Bichon Frise

size: 35 x 39

DMC	X	¼	BS
White	☆	☆	
310	■	■	╱
318	⊞	⊡	
413	◆	◆	╱
414	○	○	
415	◀	◤	
762	H	H	
792			╱
951	I	I	

BICHON FRISE

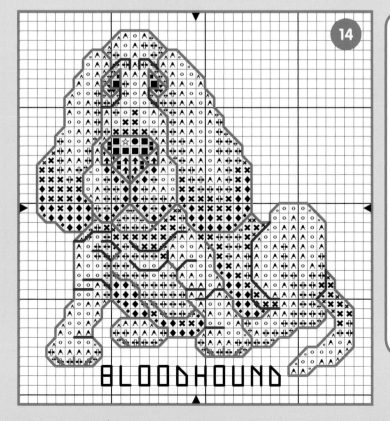

BLOODHOUND

Bloodhound

size: 34 x 37

DMC	X	¼	BS
White	☆		
310	■	■	╱
318	●		
413	↑	↑	
434	✕	✕	
435	⊞	⊡	
436	A	^	
738	○	○	
801	◆	◆	╱
3345			╱
3731		♥	

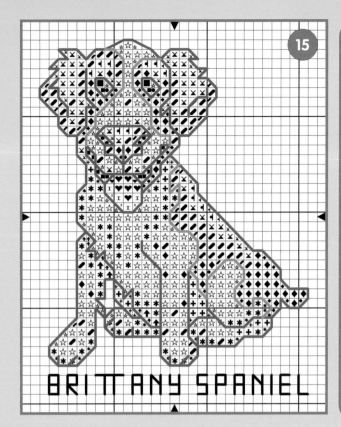

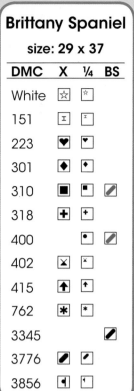

Brittany Spaniel
size: 29 x 37

DMC	X	¼	BS
White	☆	☆	
151	I	I	
223	♥	♥	
301	◆	◆	
310	■	■	⬛
318	✚	+	
400	•	•	⬛
402	⊠	⊠	
415	⬆	⬆	
762	✳	✳	
3345			⬛
3776	⬛	⬛	
3856	◖	◖	

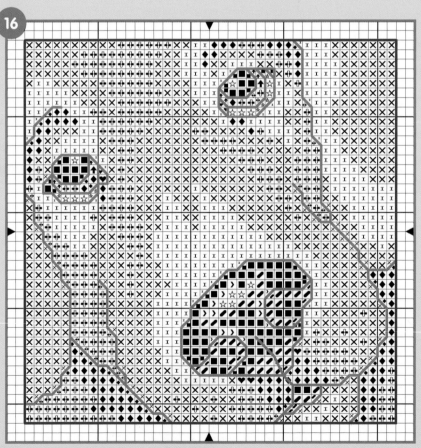

Brown Eyes
size: 40 x 40

DMC	X	¼	BS
White	☆	☆	
301	◆	◆	
310	■	■	⬛
318	❭	❭	
350	♥	♥	⬛
400	⬆	⬆	
402	⊠	⊠	
413	⬛	⬛	
3776	⊕	⊕	
3856	I	I	

Cairn Terrier

size: 30 x 39

DMC	X	¼	BS
White	☆		
223	I	I	
310	■	■	/
318	ǂ	ǂ	
400		↑	/
413	◆	◆	
414	⊙	⊙	/
415	m	m	
762	H	H	
3721	♥	♥	

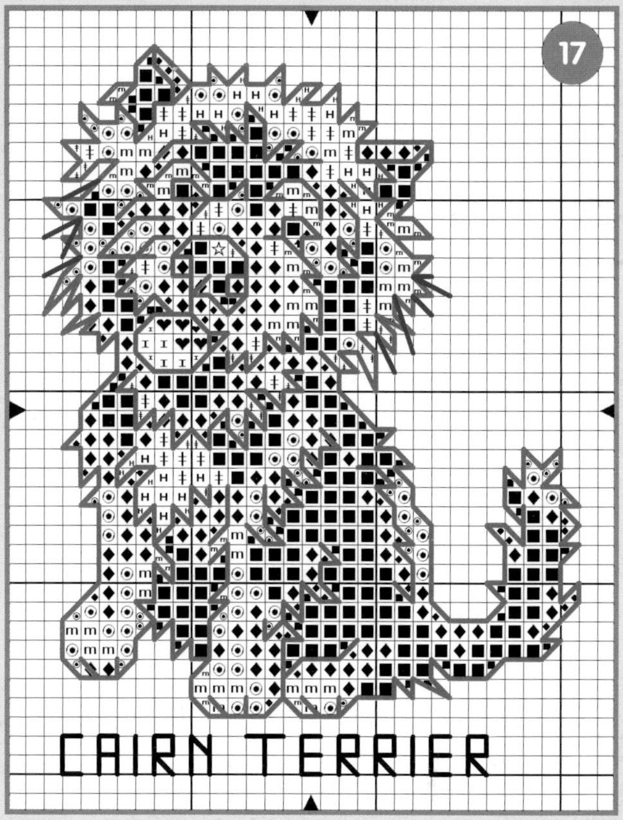

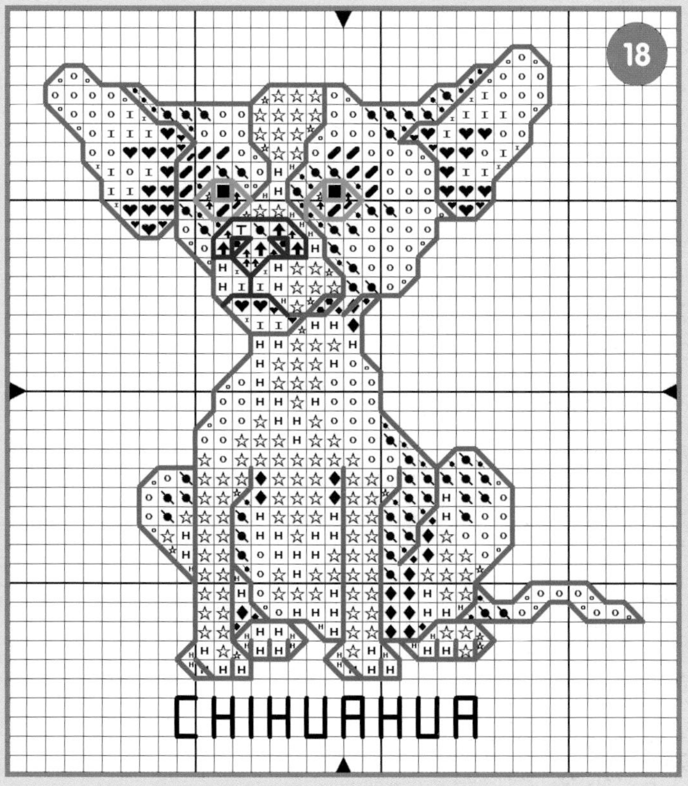

Chihuahua

size: 32 x 36

DMC	X	¼	BS
White	☆	☆	
152	I	I	
223	♥	♥	
301	↑	↑	
310	■		/
402	[illegible]	[illegible]	
413			/
415	◆	◆	
762	H	H	
801		●	/
951	T		
3345			/
3776	◢	◢	
3856	○	○	

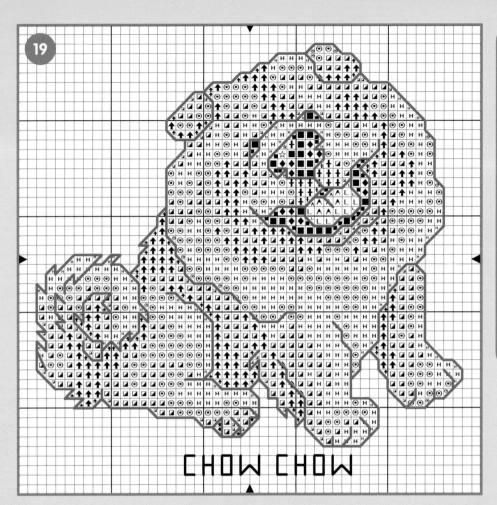

CHOW CHOW

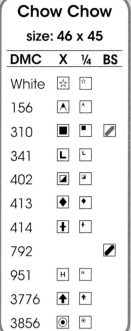

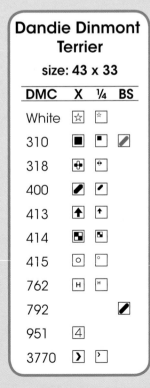

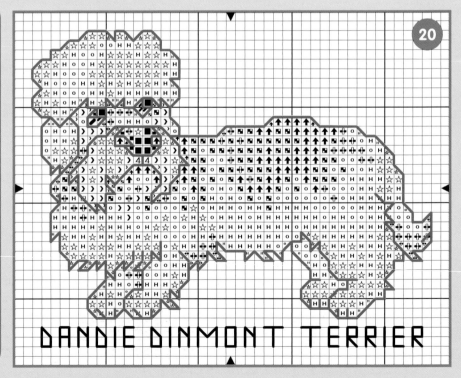

DANDIE DINMONT TERRIER

Collie

size: 44 x 39

DMC	X	¼	BS
White	☆	☆	
223	♥		
224	m		
301	⬆	⬆	
310	■	■	╱
400	⊠	⊠	
402	✖	✖	
413	◆	◆	╱
414	▣	▣	
415	◀	◀	
762	⌐	⌐	
818	I	I	
951	❭	❭	
3345			╱
3776	╱	╱	
3856	H	H	

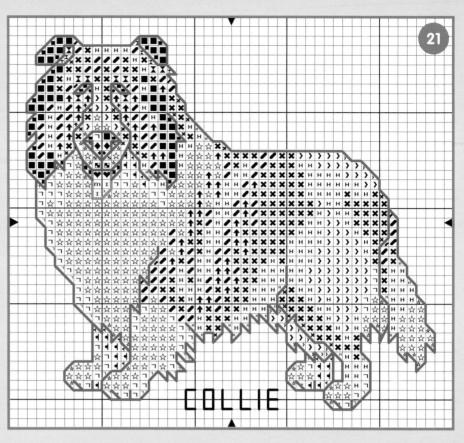

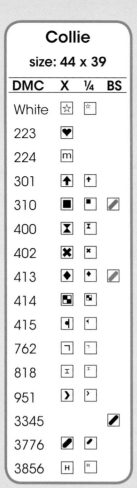

COLLIE

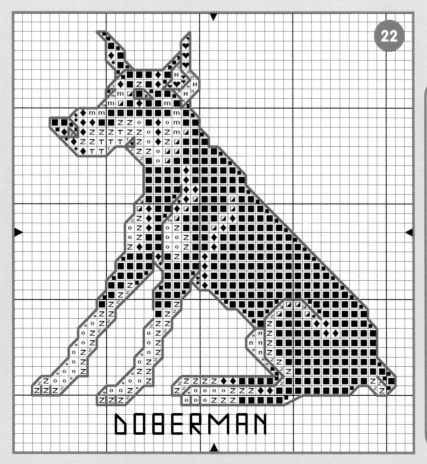

DOBERMAN

Doberman

size: 39 x 42

DMC	X	¼	BS
223	♥	♥	
224	H	H	
301	n	n	
310	■	■	╱
318	m	m	
400		◤	
402	○	○	
413	◆	◆	
414	◪	◪	
792			╱
3776	Z	Z	
3856	T	T	

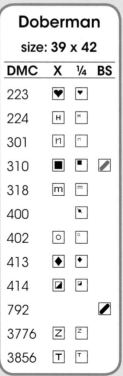

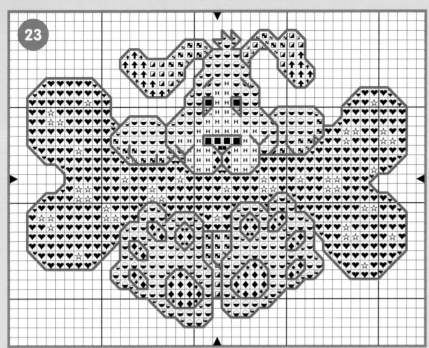

Dog Bone
size: 41 x 31

DMC	X	¼	BS
White	☆		
301	◩	◪	
310	■	◧	╱
350	♥	♥	
402	◖	◗	
414	◆	◆	
801	↑	↑	
3776	◪	◪	
3856	H	H	

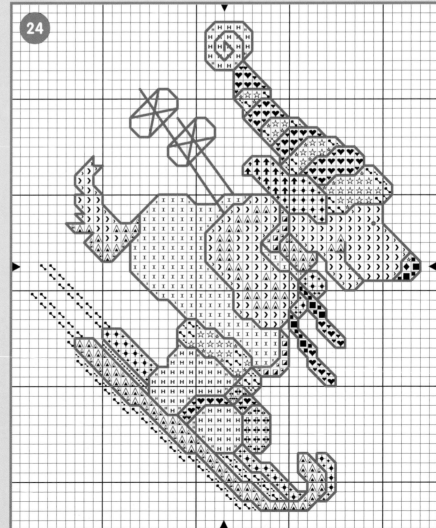

Downhill Dog
size: 42 x 51

DMC	X	¼	BS	FK
White	☆	☆		
208	✦	✦		
209	H	H		
301	↑	↑		
310	■	◧	╱	●
350	♥	♥		
402	◭	◭		
413	◆			
702	◩	◪		
907	I	I		
3747	◣	◞		
3776	✦	✦		
3856	❭	❭		

English Setter
size: 44 x 32

DMC	X	¼	BS
White	☆	☆	
151	I	I	
223	♥		
310		■	╱
318	◣	◣	
356	◪	◪	
413			╱
414	◆	◆	
415	n	n	
758	H	H	
762	❯	❯	
3345			╱
3721	✖	✗	
3777	⬆	⬆	
3778	A	^	
3830	L	L	

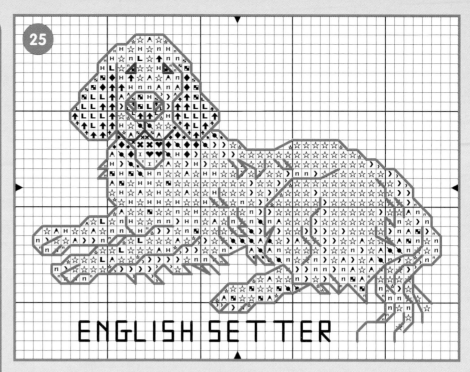

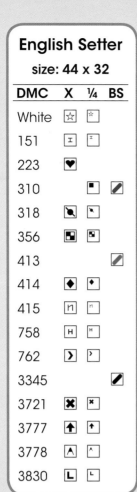

ENGLISH SETTER

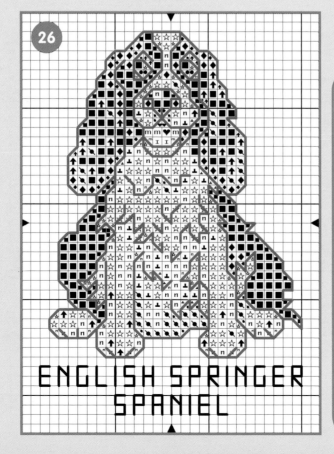

ENGLISH SPRINGER SPANIEL

English Springer Spaniel
size: 28 x 44

DMC	X	¼	BS
White	☆	☆	
151	I		
223	m	m	
310	■	■	╱
318	◣	◣	
400		▪	
413	◆	◆	
414	⬆	⬆	
415	⊥	⊥	
762	n	n	
3721	♥	♥	╱

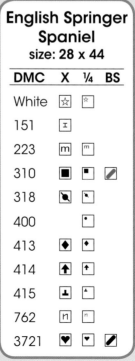

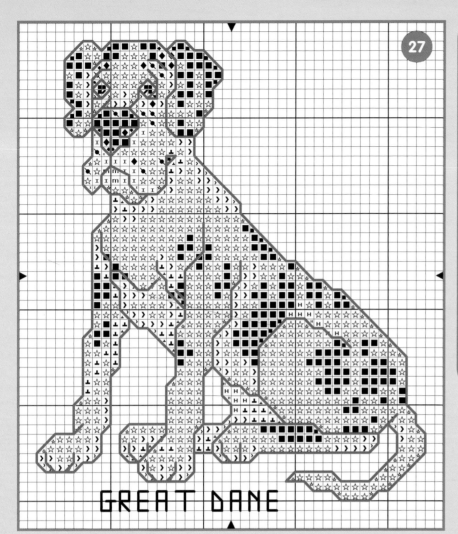

GREAT DANE

Great Dane
size: 42 x 49

DMC	X	¼	BS
White	☆	☆	
223	m		
224	I	I	
310	■	■	⟋
318	⊥	⊥	
400		⟋	
413	◆	◆	
414	◥	◢	
415	H	H	
762	❭	❭	
3345			⟋
3731	♥		

Jack Russell Terrier
size: 37 x 36

DMC	X	¼	BS
White	☆	☆	
301	↑	↑	
310	■	■	⟋
318	✚	✚	
402	◼	◼	
413	◆		
415	H	H	
762	❭	❭	
3345			⟋
3776	Z	Z	

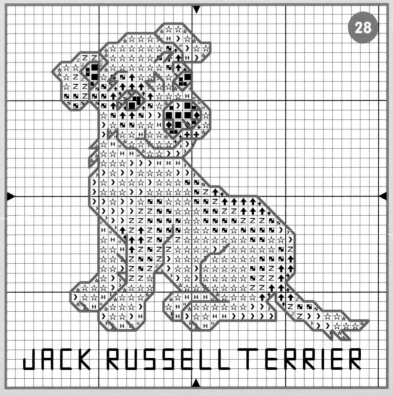

JACK RUSSELL TERRIER

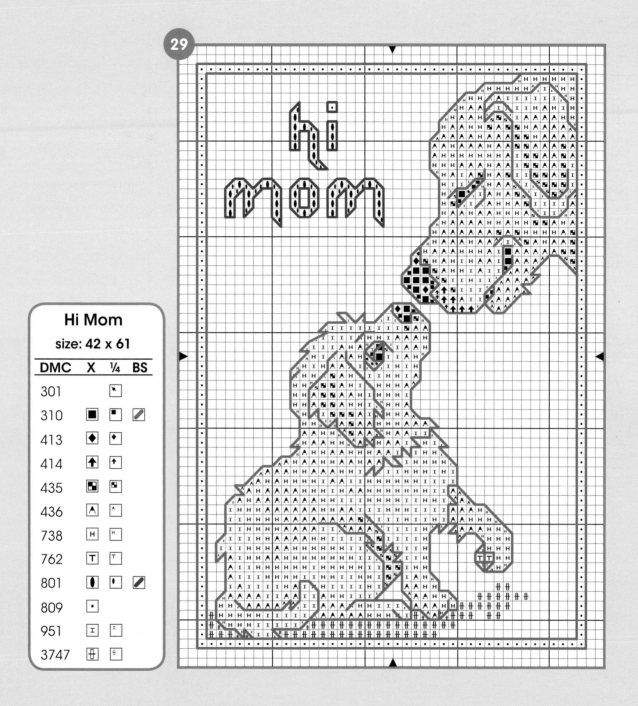

Hi Mom

size: 42 x 61

DMC	X	¼	BS
301		◣	
310	■	◪	▨
413	◆	◆	
414	↟	↑	
435	◪	◪	
436	◿	◿	
738	H	H	
762	T	T	
801	◖	◖	▨
809	·		
951	I	I	
3747	⊞	⊞	

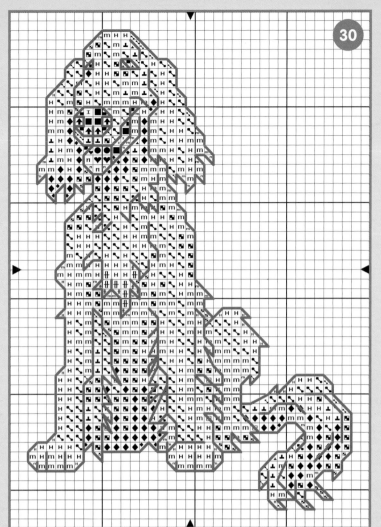

30

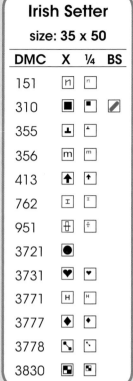

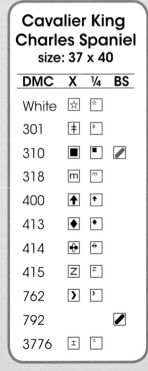

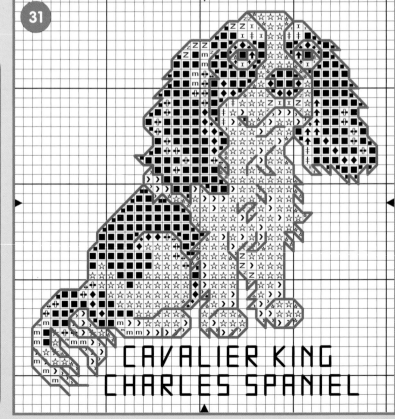

31

CAVALIER KING
CHARLES SPANIEL

Little Dog

size: 41 x 42

DMC	X	¼	BS
White	☆		
310	■	▪	╱
318	m	ᵐ	
413	◆	◆	
415	❯		
435	↑	↑	
436	◪	◪	
738	4	4	
951	⌐	⌐	
3607	♥	♥	
3608	T	T	

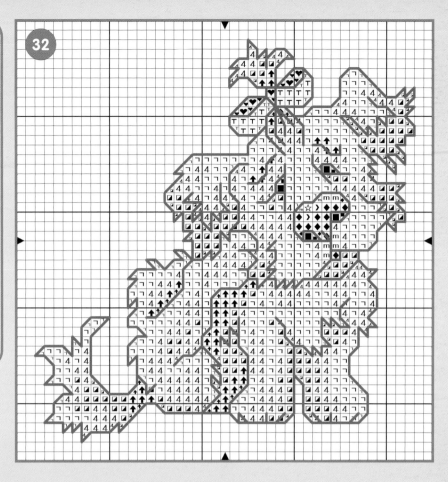

32

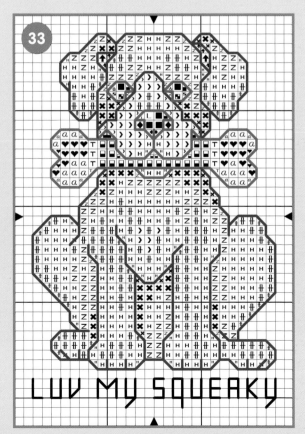

33

LUV MY SQUEAKY

Luv My Squeaky

size: 26 x 39

DMC	X	¼	BS
White		☆	
208	◪	◪	
310	■	▪	╱
350	♥	♥	╱
400	◪	◪	
413	◆	◆	
434	✖	✖	
435	Z	ᶻ	
436	H	ᴴ	
702	T	T	
721	a	ᵃ	
738	⧣	⧣	
739	❯	❯	
762	⌐	⌐	
801	↑	↑	╱

MALTESE

Maltese
size: 36 x 38

DMC	X	¼	BS
White	☆	☆	
151	�		
223	✚	✚	
224	I	I	
310	■	■	╱
318	▣	▣	
400		⊥	
413	◆		╱
414	↑	↑	
415	◥	◥	
762	H	H	
3721	♥	♥	╱
3731	✦	✦	
3776	✚		

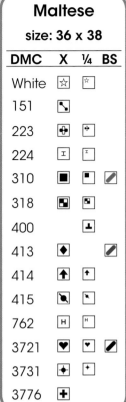

Don't Mess with Me
size: 38 x 45

DMC	X	¼	BS	FK
White	☆	☆		●
151	L	L		
301	✖	✖		
310	■	■	╱	●
318	◣	◣		
413	◆	◆		
435	✦	✦		
436	H	H		
762	I	I		
801	↑	↑		
951	❭	❭		
3731	♥	♥		
3733	m	m		

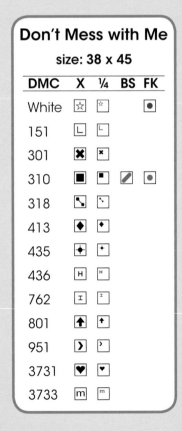

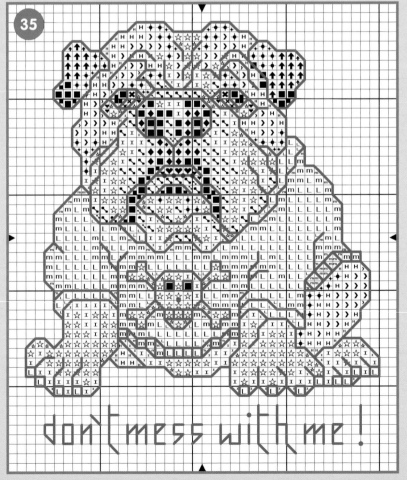

don't mess with me!

Mutt-a-Tude

size: 38 x 48

DMC	X	¼	BS
White	☆	☆	
151	H	H	
223	◆	◆	
301	✦	✦	
310	■	■	╱
350	✕	✕	╱
413	❶	❶	
415	m	m	
762	〉	〉	
792	⬆	⬆	
839	◆	◆	╱
840	⊞	⊞	
841	◥	◥	
842	L	L	
3721	♥	♥	╱

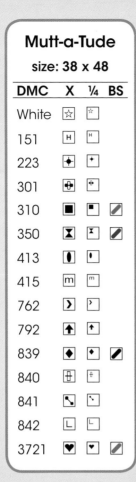

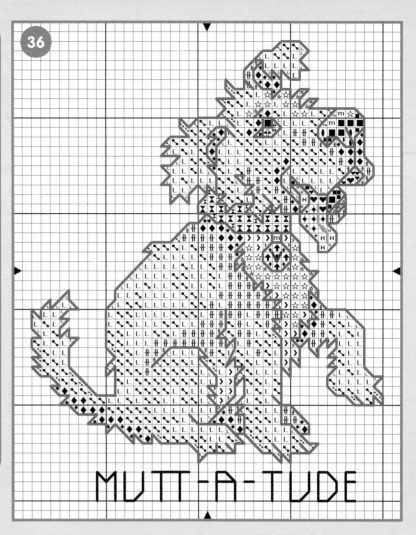

36

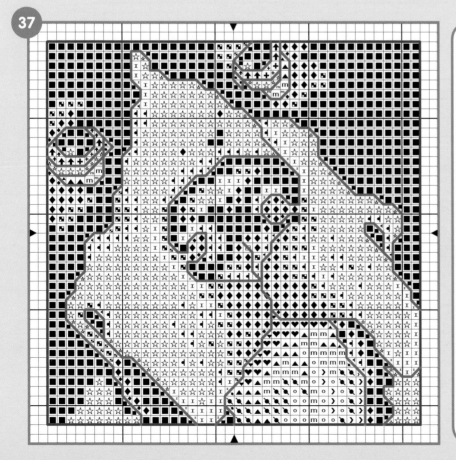

37

Newf Face

size: 40 x 40

DMC	X	¼	BS
White	☆	☆	
151	○		
223	m	m	
310	■	■	╱
318	◀	◀	
400	⬆	⬆	
413	◆	◆	
414	◪	◪	
762	I	I	
816	♥	♥	
818	〉	〉	
3721	▲	▲	
3731	◣	◣	
3776	✚	✚	╱

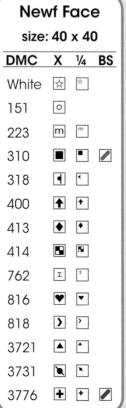

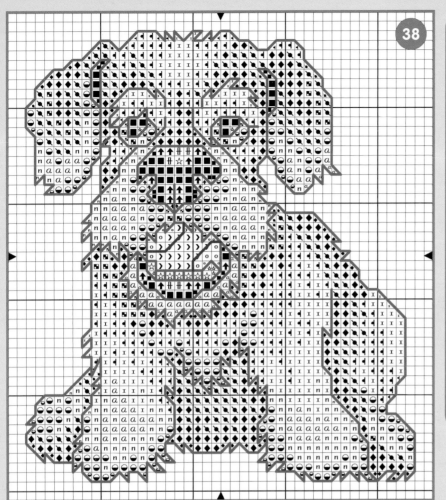

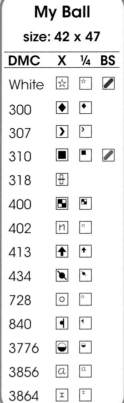

My Ball

size: 42 x 47

DMC	X	¼	BS
White	☆	☆	/
300	◆	◆	
307	⟩	⟩	
310	■	■	/
318	⊞		
400	◩	◨	
402	n	n	
413	▲	▲	
434	◣	◢	
728	○	○	
840	◀	◀	
3776	◐	◐	
3856	a	a	
3864	I	I	

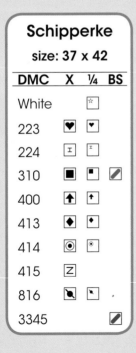

Schipperke

size: 37 x 42

DMC	X	¼	BS
White		☆	
223	♥	♥	
224	I	I	
310	■	■	/
400	▲	▲	
413	◆	◆	
414	◉	◉	
415	Z		
816	◣	◢	
3345			/

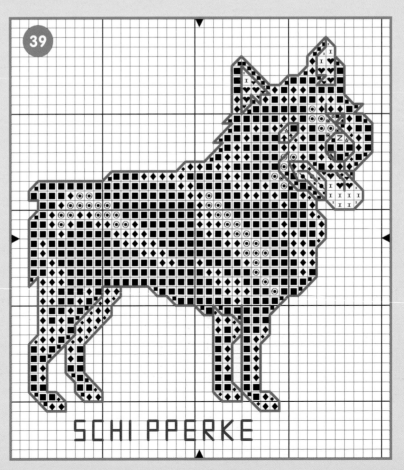

SCHIPPERKE

Sheltie

size: 43 x 40

DMC	X	¼	BS
White	☆	☆	
151	○	○	
301		↑	
310	■	■	▧
318	‡	‡	
402	▲	^	
413	◆	◆	
702	▮	▮	
742	◣	◤	
744	L	L	
762	❯	❯	
907	n	n	
996	✚	✚	
3776	△	△	
3846	H	H	
3856	⊞	⊞	

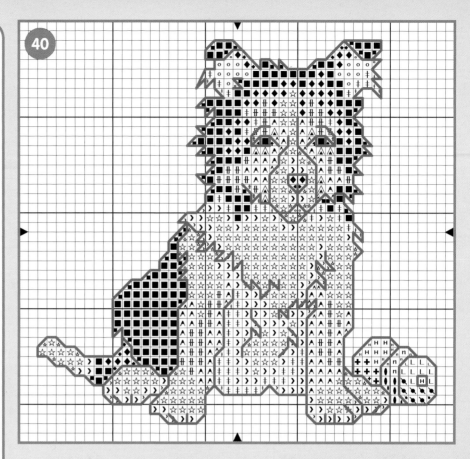

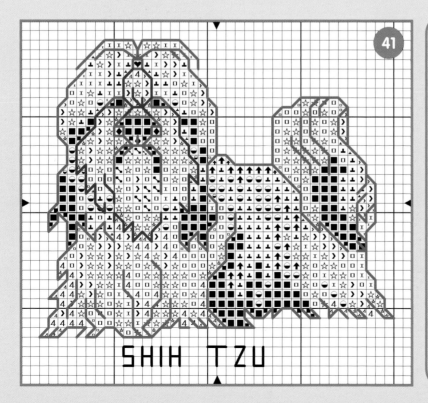

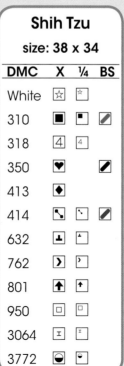

SHIH TZU

Shih Tzu

size: 38 x 34

DMC	X	¼	BS
White	☆	☆	
310	■	■	▧
318	4	4	
350	♥		▧
413	◆		
414	◥	◥	▧
632	⊥	⊥	
762	❯	❯	
801	↑	↑	
950	□	□	
3064	ɪ	ɪ	
3772	◓	◓	

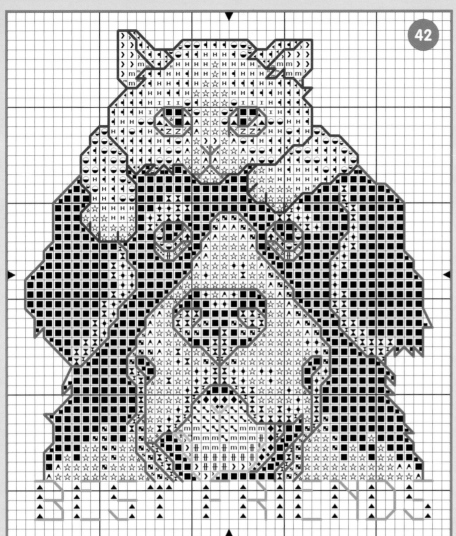

Newf & Friend

size: 44 x 51

DMC	X	¼	BS
White	☆	☆	
151	⊞	⊞	
224	m	m	
310	■	■	╱
318	◨	◨	
400	↑	↑	╱
402	◁	◁	
413	⊠	⊠	
414	✦	✦	
702	▲	▲	╱
762	Ａ	Ａ	
815	◆	◆	
818	❭	❭	
907	Z	Z	
951	I	I	
3721			╱
3731	◣	◥	╱
3776	◒	◒	
3856	H	H	

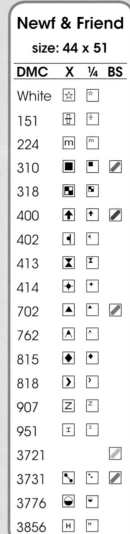

Shar-Pei

size: 38 x 35

DMC	X	¼	BS	FK
310	■	■	╱	
413	◆	◆		
414	◪	◪		
434	↑	↑	╱	
435	★	★		
436	⊥	⊥		
738	Ａ	Ａ		
739	⊞	⊞		
762	○			
792	♥	♥	╱	●
809	T	T		
951	❭	❭		

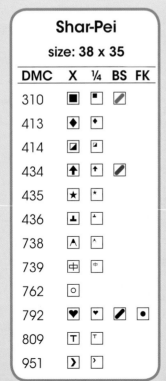

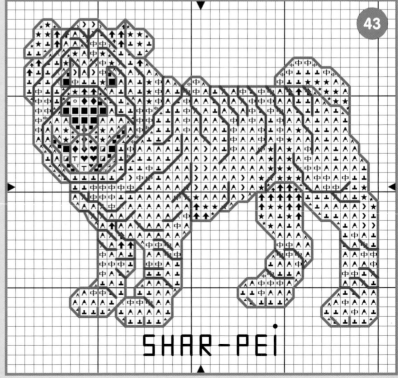

SHAR-PEi

Rotten Dogs

size: 48 x 51

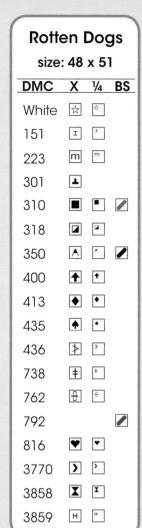

DMC	X	¼	BS
White	☆	☆	
151	I	I	
223	m	m	
301	⊥		
310	■	■	⁄
318	◩	◩	
350	◮	^	⁄
400	⬆	↑	
413	◆	◆	
435	♠	♠	
436	ⶠ	ⶠ	
738	‡	‡	
762	⊞	⊞	
792			⁄
816	♥	♥	
3770	❭	❭	
3858	⊠	I	
3859	H	H	

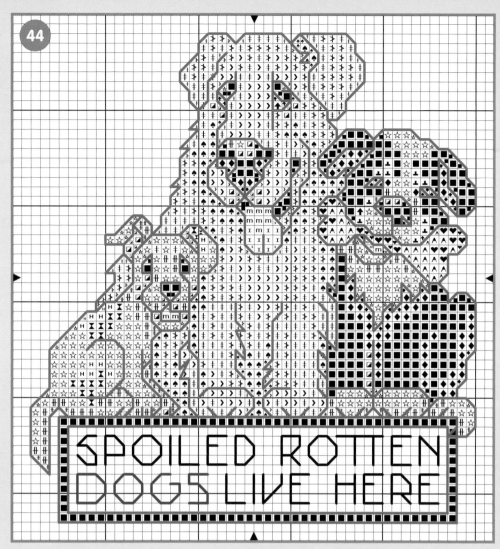

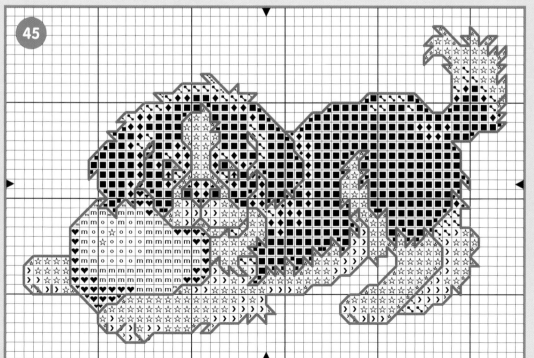

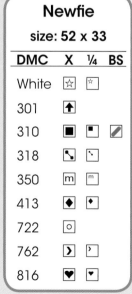

Newfie

size: 52 x 33

DMC	X	¼	BS
White	☆	☆	
301	⬆		
310	■	■	⁄
318	◥	◥	
350	m	m	
413	◆	◆	
722	○		
762	❭	❭	
816	♥	♥	

27

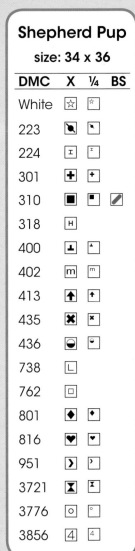

Shepherd Pup

size: 34 x 36

DMC	X	¼	BS
White	☆	☆	
223	◣	◤	
224	I	I	
301	✛	+	
310	■	■	╱
318	H		
400	⊥	⊥	
402	m	m	
413	↑	↑	
435	✖	✖	
436	◓	◓	
738	L		
762	□		
801	◆	◆	
816	♥	♥	
951	❯	❯	
3721	✕	✕	
3776	o	o	
3856	4	4	

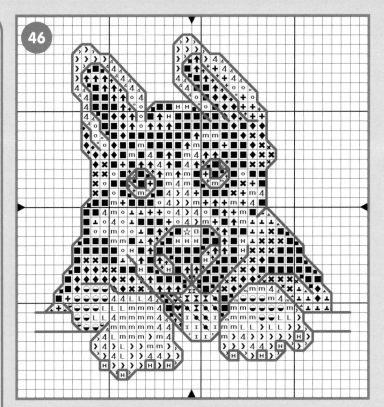

46

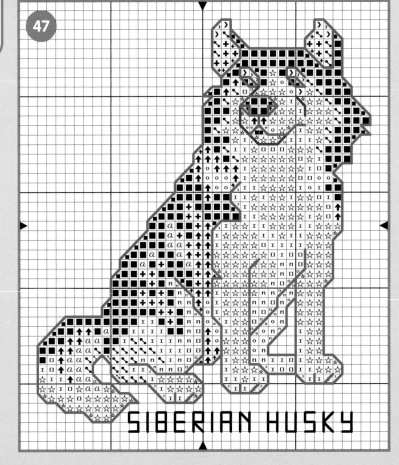

47

SIBERIAN HUSKY

Siberian Husky

size: 36 x 43

DMC	X	¼	BS
White	☆	☆	
310	■	■	╱
318	n	n	
413	↑	↑	
414	o	o	╱
415	□	□	
739	◥	◥	
762	I	I	
792			╱
809		•	
840	✛	+	
841	@	@	
3770	❯	❯	

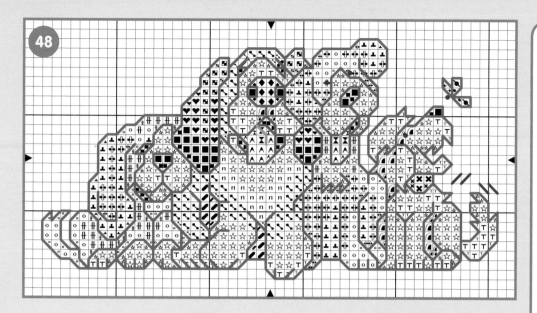

Puppy Love

size: 49 x 25

DMC	X	¼	BS	FK
White	☆	☆		
151	A	^		
223	⊠	⊡		
301	◪	◪		
310	■	■	◪	•
318	◩	◩		
350	✖	×		
400	♥	♥		
402	◥	◥		
413	◆	◆	◪	
435	⊥	⊥		
436	⊞	⊞		
722		+		
738	○	○		
739	⊞	⊞		
743	◩	◩		
762	T	T		
3721			◪	
3776	▣	▣		
3856	n	n		

Smile

size: 31 x 39

DMC	X	¼	BS	FK
White	☆	☆		
223	◥	◥		
224	⊡	⊡		
310	■	■	◪	
318	◥	◥		
350	⊠	⊡	◪	•
400		×		
413	↟	↑		
415	n	n	◪	
435	L	L		
436	○	○		
762	⟩	⟩		
3731	♥	♥		
3776	◆	◆		

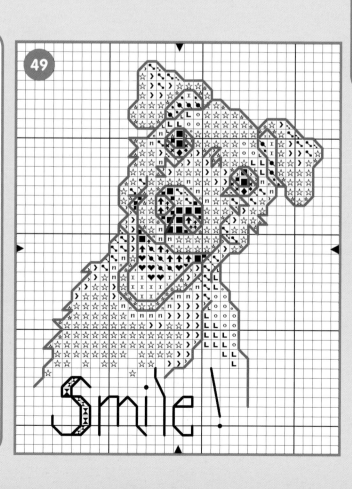

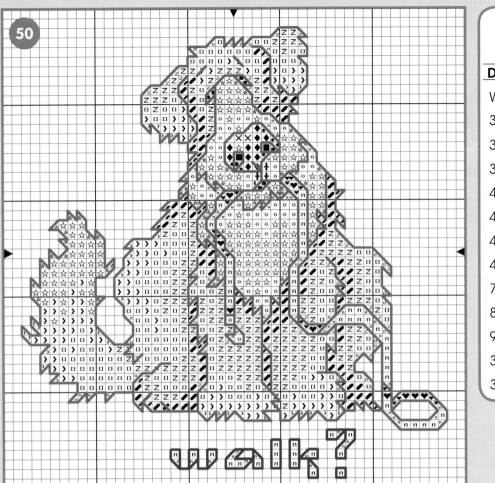

50

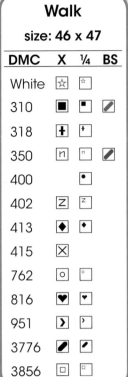

Walk
size: 46 x 47

DMC	X	¼	BS
White	☆	☆	
310	■	■	╱
318	✚	✚	
350	n	n	╱
400		•	
402	Z	Z	
413	◆	◆	
415	✕		
762	○	○	
816	♥	♥	
951	❯	❯	
3776	╱	╱	
3856	▢	▢	

Welsh Corgi
size: 49 x 32

DMC	X	¼	BS
White	☆	☆	
151	I	I	
223	⬆		
301	●	•	
310	■	■	╱
318	H	H	
413	◆		
435	✖	✖	
436	L	L	
738	T	T	
762	○	○	
792			╱
801	❘	•	
951	❯	❯	
3721	♥		

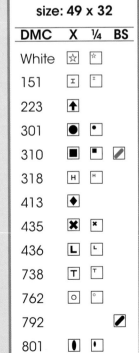

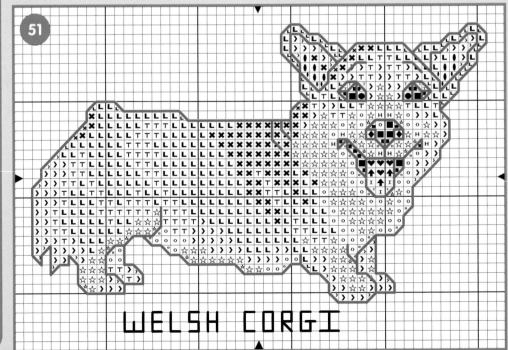

51

Welcome

size: 38 x 69

DMC	X	¼	BS
White	☆		
301	✖	✗	
307	H	H	
310	■	■	✎
402	Z	Z	
413	◆	◆	
604	♥	♥	
704	○	○	
801	▲	▲	
3776	L	L	
3844			✎
3846	A	A	
3856	I	I	

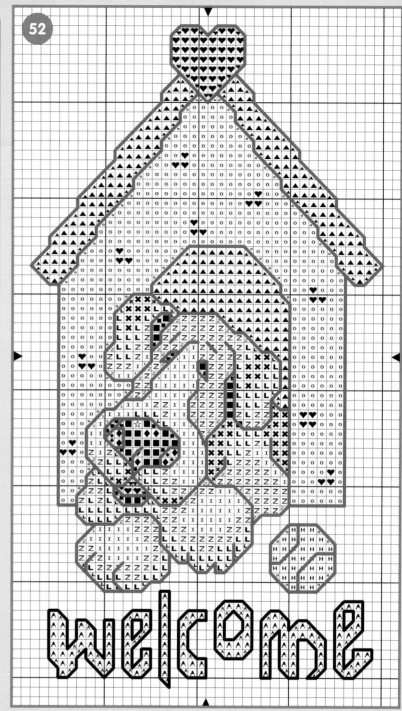

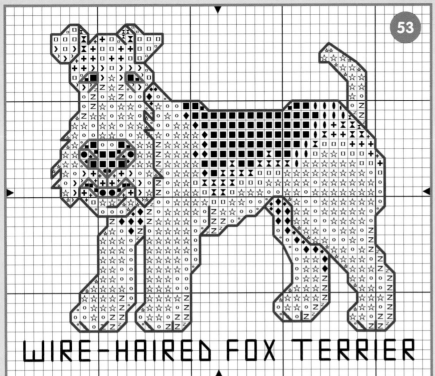

WIRE-HAIRED FOX TERRIER

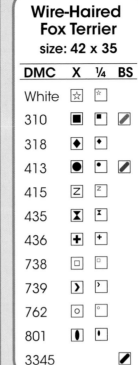

Wire-Haired Fox Terrier
size: 42 x 35

DMC	X	¼	BS
White	☆	☆	
310	■	▪	/
318	◆	◆	/
413	●	•	/
415	Z	z	
435	✕	✕	
436	✦	✦	
738	▢	▫	
739	❭	❯	
762	○	○	
801	◗	◖	
3345			/

Yorkshire Terrier
size: 41 x 39

DMC	X	¼	BS
White	☆	☆	
310	■	▪	/
350	n	n	
400	●		
402	H	H	
413	◆	◆	
414	▢	▫	
415	L	L	
435	✦	✦	/
436	‡		
801	/	/	
816	▲	▴	
951	❭	❯	
3345			/
3776	▣	▣	
3856	○	○	

YORKSHIRE TERRIER

American Curl

size: 30 x 39

DMC	X	¼	BS
White	☆		
310	■	◼	╱
435	♠	♠	
436	⊕	⊕	
738	◓	◓	
792	◆		╱
801	◨	◨	
809	m	m	
839	◨	◨	
840	⊠	⊠	
951	H	H	
3757	‡		

AMERICAN CURL

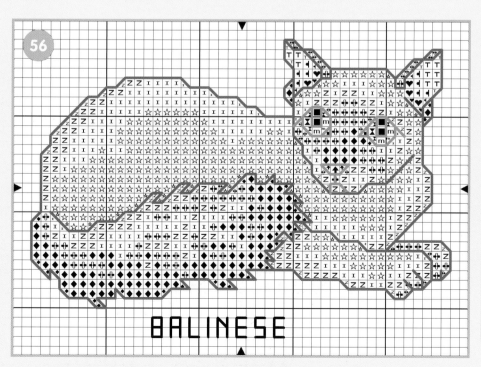

BALINESE

Balinese

size: 45 x 31

DMC	X	¼	BS
White	☆	☆	
159	Z	Z	
160	⊕	⊕	
161	◆	◆	
223	◀	◀	
310	■	◼	╱
413	♠	♠	╱
762	I	I	
818	T	T	
995	⊠	⊠	╱
996	m	m	
3721	♥	♥	

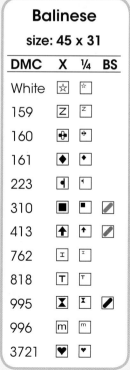

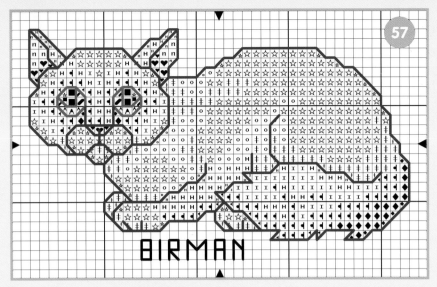

BIRMAN

Birman
size: 41 x 24

DMC	X	¼	BS
White	☆	☆	
151	n	n	
152	♥	♥	
310	■	■	╱
402	◀	◀	
413			╱
762	‡	‡	
792	▨	▨	╱
809	A	^	
951	I	I	
3770	○	○	
3776	◆	◆	
3856	H	H	

British Shorthair
size: 31 x 38

DMC	X	¼	BS
White	☆	☆	
223	♥	♥	
301	↑	↑	
310	■		╱
400	◆	◆	
402	Z	Z	
742	✕	✕	
743	n	n	
762	○	○	
792			╱
801			╱
3721	◣	◣	
3776	◉	◉	
3856	I	I	

BRITISH SHORTHAIR

Burmese

size: 32 x 40

DMC	X	¼	BS
White		☆	
223	ꞮꞮ	Ɪ	
310	■	▪	◿
434	m	m	
435	Z	z	
742	T	T	
782	◣	◢	
801	↑	↑	
938	◆	◆	
996			◿
3721	♥	♥	

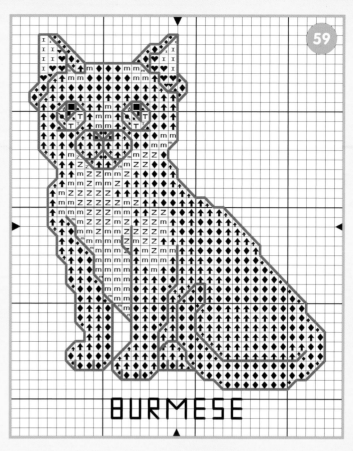

59

BURMESE

60

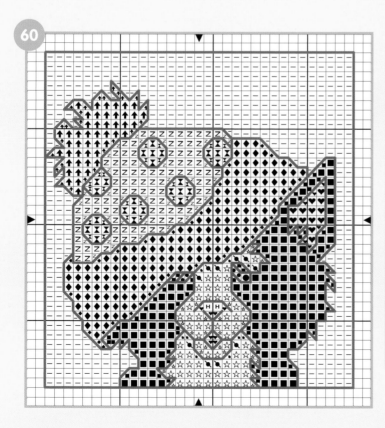

Cat Hat

size: 33 x 35

DMC	X	¼	BS
White	☆	☆	
151	H		
208	↑	↑	
310	■	▪	◿
350	◆	◆	
743	─	─	
762	◣	◢	
907	●	▪	
955	Z	z	
3731	♥	♥	
3846	⨉	⨉	

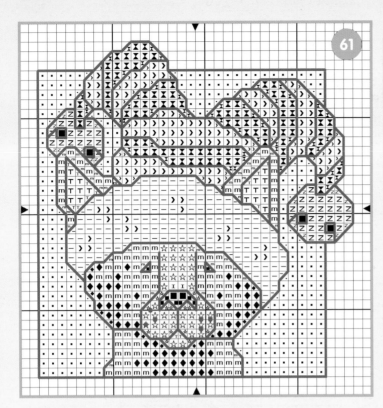

61

Cat Hat 2

size: 34 x 35

DMC	X	¼	BS	FK
White	☆	☆		
151	T	T		
209	❭	❭		
310	■	■	╱	●
350	·	·		
414	◆	◆		
415	m	m		
604	✕	✕		
762	I			
954	−	−		
3821	Z	z		

Cat Hat 3

size: 33 x 36

DMC	X	¼	BS	FK
White	☆	☆		
208	↑	↑		
209	−	−		
310	■		╱	●
604	H	H		
721	◆	◆		
722	m	m		
762	I	I		
951	❭	❭		
954	4	4		
3846	·	·		

62

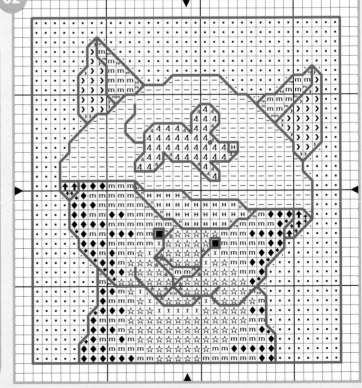

Cat Hat 4

size: 33 x 37

DMC	X	¼	BS
209	I	I	
310	■		◢
350	⊥	⊥	
722	Z	Z	
801	◆	◆	
816	♥	♥	
907	·	·	
951	O	○	
996	❘		
3779	m	m	
3858	⬆	⬆	
3859	▣	▣	

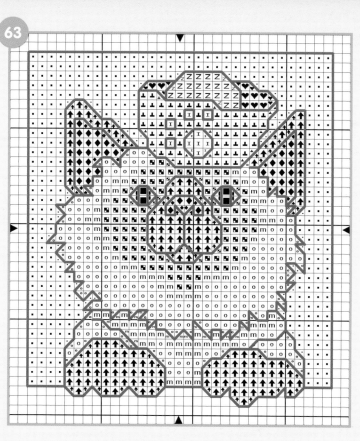

63

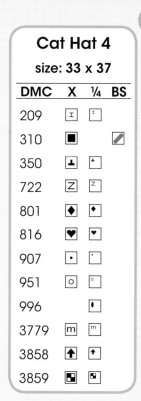

64

Cat's Motto

size: 36 x 52

DMC	X	¼	BS	FK
223	⬆	⬆		
224	Z	Z		
310	■		◢	
434	✚	✚		
435	♥	♥		
436	I	I		
792			◢	●
801	◆		◢	●
951	4	4		
3770	H	H		

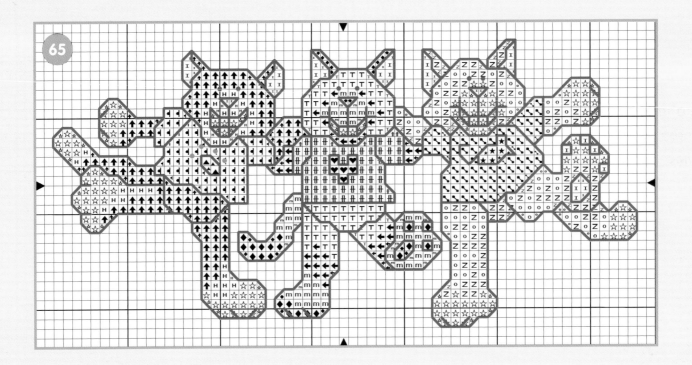

Dancing Cats

size: 63 x 30

DMC	X	¼	BS	FK
White	☆	☆		
151	I	I		
209	⊞	⊞		
350	♥			
310			◨	●
414	⬆	⬆		
434	m	m		
435	⬅	⬅		
722	Z	Z		
743	▲	▲		●
762	H	H		
801	◆	◆		
907	◣	◟		
951	T	T		
3608	★	★		
3776	o	o		
3846	◀	◀		

Exotic Longhair

size: 40 x 42

DMC	X	¼	BS
White	☆	☆	
310	■	■	/
318	m	m	
402	◨	◩	
413	◆	◆	/
414	◪	◪	
721	⬆	⬆	
722	◀	◀	
762	o	o	
951	❭	❭	
3345			/
3856	H	H	

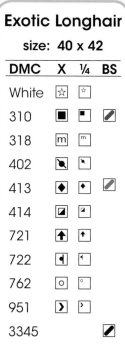

Cats Believe

size: 24 x 64

DMC	X	¼	BS	FK
White	☆	☆		
151	I	I		
310			/	
762	H	H		
792			/	●
816			/	●
922	⬆	⬆		
3731	♥	♥		
3825	o	o		

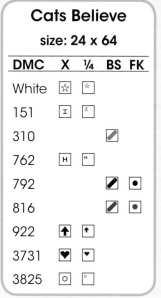

67

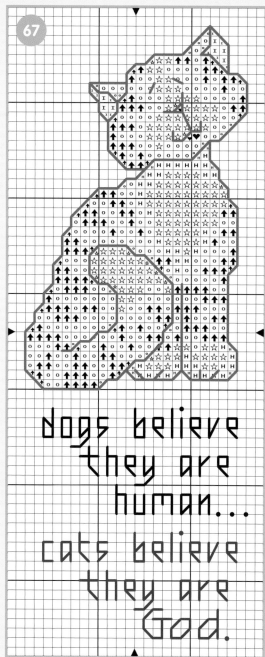

66

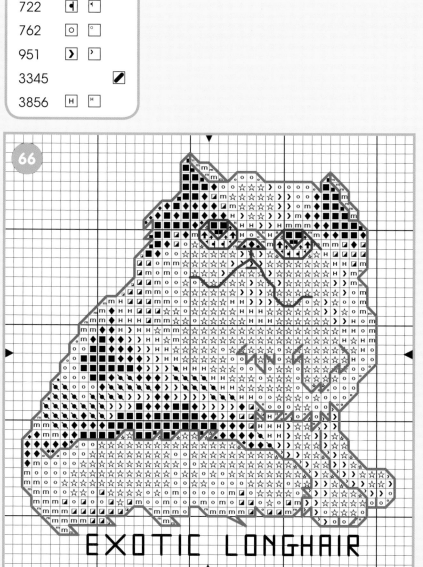

EXOTIC LONGHAIR

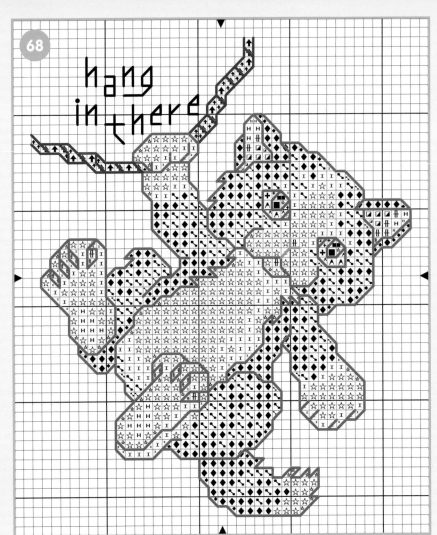

hang
in there

Hang in There
size: 41 x 50

DMC	X	¼	BS	FK
White	☆	☆		
151	⊞	⊞		
223	◨	◨		
310	■	■	⟋	
318	◰	◰		
414	◆	◆		
436	▲	▲		
762	I	I		
798	✚	✚	⟋	●
801			⟋	
809	A	A		
818	H	H		
3721			⟋	

Kitty
size: 34 x 42

DMC	X	¼	BS
White	☆	☆	
151	❭	❭	
223	m	m	
310	■	■	⟋
762	Z	Z	
816			♥
922	◥	◥	
3825	I	I	

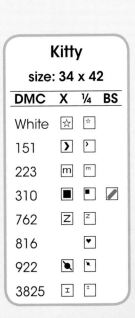

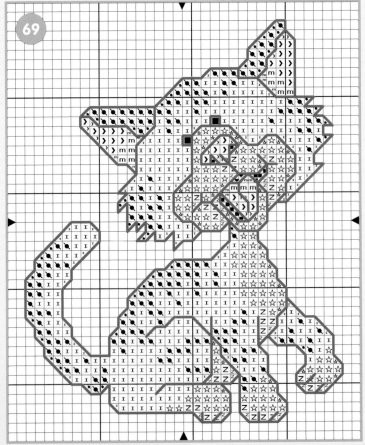

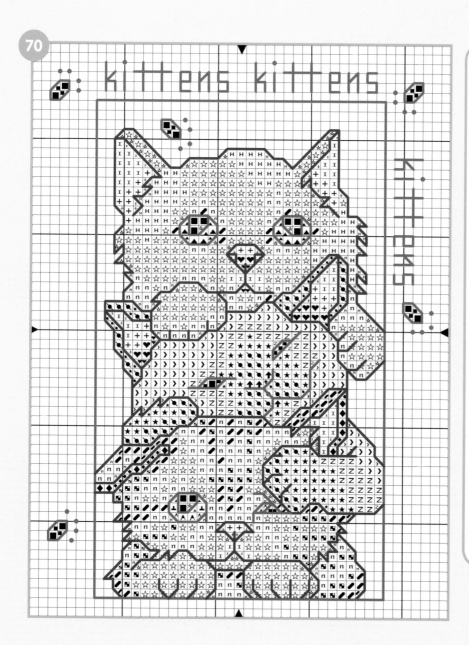

Kittens

size: 41 x 56

DMC	X	¼	BS	FK
White	☆	☆		
151	⊞	⊞		
223	♥	♥		
310	■	■	▨	⊡
318	◪	◪		
413	◆	◆	▨	
415	◧	◧		
702	⊥	⊥		
762	n	n		
801	⬆	⬆		
818	I	I		
907	◬	◬		
3770	❭	❭		
3779	Z	Z		
3846	▲	▲		
3856	H	H		
3858	◨	◨		
3859	★	★		

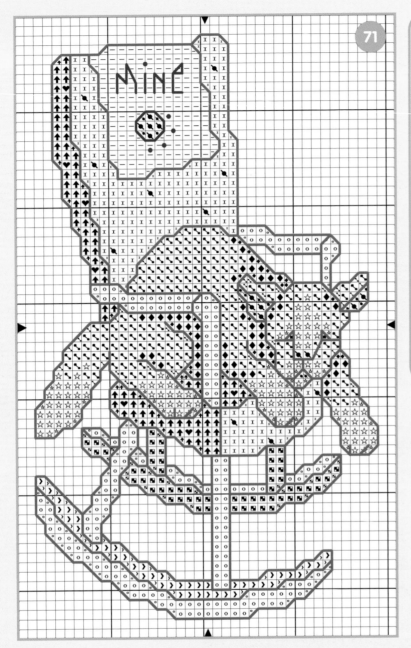

Mine

size: 37 x 61

DMC	X	¼	BS	FK
White	☆	☆		
151	◨	◨		
318	◆	◆		
310		■	╱	
368	↑	↑		
369	I	I		
402	◧	◧		
415	◣	◟		
951	❭	❭		
964	—	—		
3731	♥		╱	●
3856	○	○		

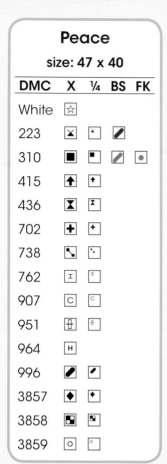

Peace

size: 47 x 40

DMC	X	¼	BS	FK
White	☆			
223	☒	☒	◩	
310	■	■	◩	●
415	⬆	⬆		
436	⊠	⊠		
702	✚	✚		
738	◥	◥		
762	I	I		
907	C	C		
951	⊞	⊞		
964	H			
996	◪	◪		
3857	◆	◆		
3858	◨	◨		
3859	○	○		

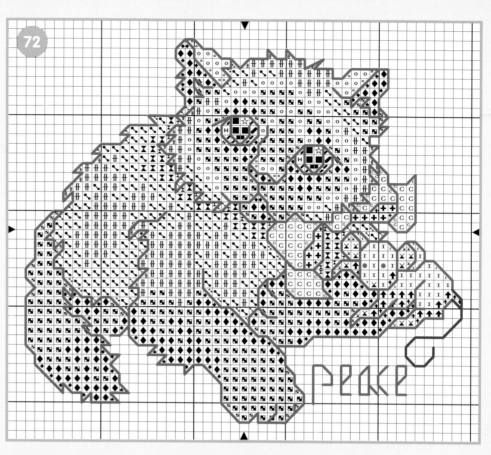

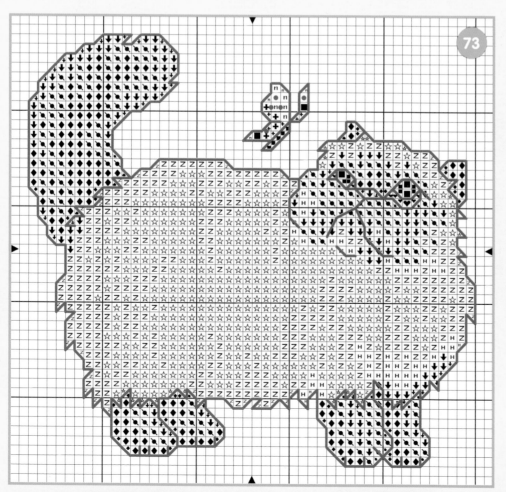

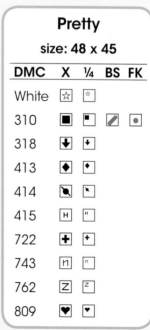

Pretty

size: 48 x 45

DMC	X	¼	BS	FK
White	☆	☆		
310	■	■	◩	●
318	⬇	⬇		
413	◆	◆		
414	◩	◩		
415	H	H		
722	✚	✚		
743	n	n		
762	Z	Z		
809	♥	♥		

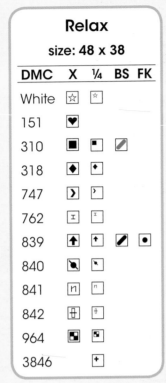

Relax

size: 48 x 38

DMC	X	¼	BS	FK
White	☆	☆		
151	♥			
310	■	▪	◨	
318	◆	◆		
747	〉	〉		
762	I	I		
839	↑	↑	◨	●
840	◣	◣		
841	n	n		
842	⊞	⊞		
964	◪	◪		
3846		✚		

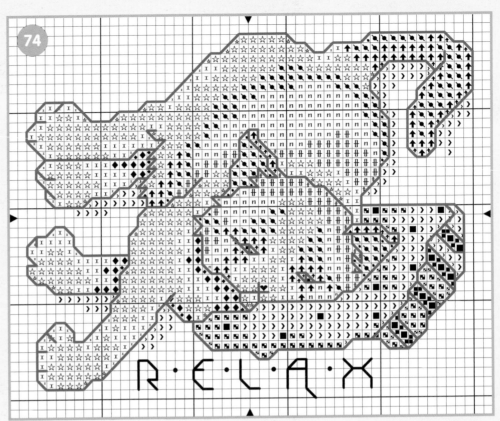

74

R·E·L·A·X

75

there are cat people...

··and everybody else··

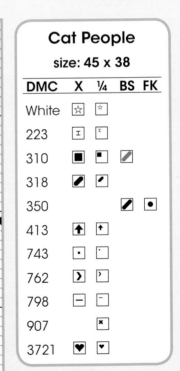

Cat People

size: 45 x 38

DMC	X	¼	BS	FK
White	☆	☆		
223	I	I		
310	■	▪	◨	
318	◨	◨		
350			◨	●
413	↑	↑		
743	·	·		
762	〉	〉		
798	—	—		
907		✕		
3721	♥	♥		

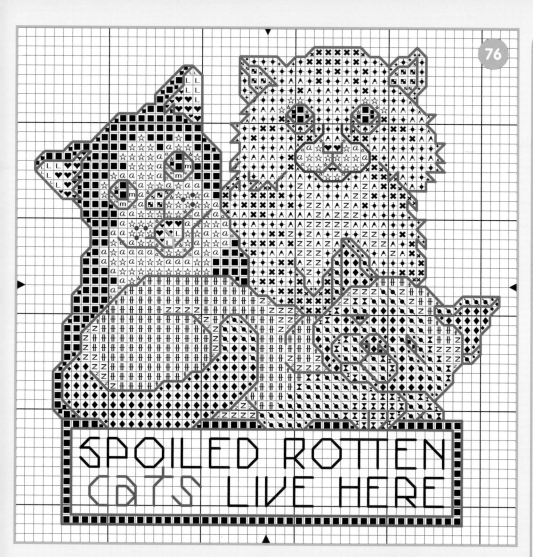

Rotten Cats

size: 50 x 50

DMC	X	¼	BS	FK
White	☆	☆		
151	L	L		
223	♥	♥		
224	▣	▣		
310	■	■	╱	
350			╱	
402	✦	✦		
414			╱	•
743	m	m		.
762	ⓐ	ⓐ		
792			╱	
907	♠	♠		
951	Z	Z		
3770	⊞	⊞		
3776	✖	✖		
3856	A	A		
3857	◆	◆		
3858	◥	◥	╱	
3859	✕	✕		

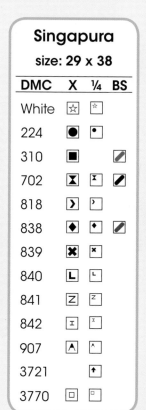

Singapura

size: 29 x 38

DMC	X	¼	BS
White	☆	☆	
224	●	•	
310	■		╱
702	✕	✕	╱
818	❭	❭	
838	◆	◆	╱
839	✖	✖	
840	L	L	
841	Z	Z	
842	I	I	
907	A	A	
3721		↟	
3770	▢	▢	

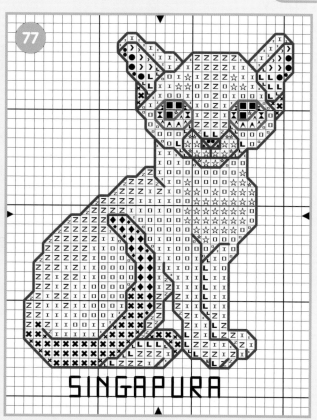

SINGAPURA

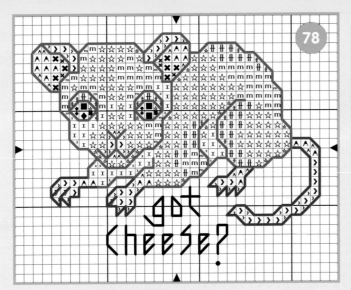

Got Cheese

size: 31 x 24

DMC	X	¼	BS	FK
White	☆	☆		
151	A	^		
223	✖	✖		
310	■	■	╱	
318	m	m		
400	◆	◆		
415	⊞	⊞		
721			╱	●
762	I	I		
818	⟩	⟩		
3731			╱	

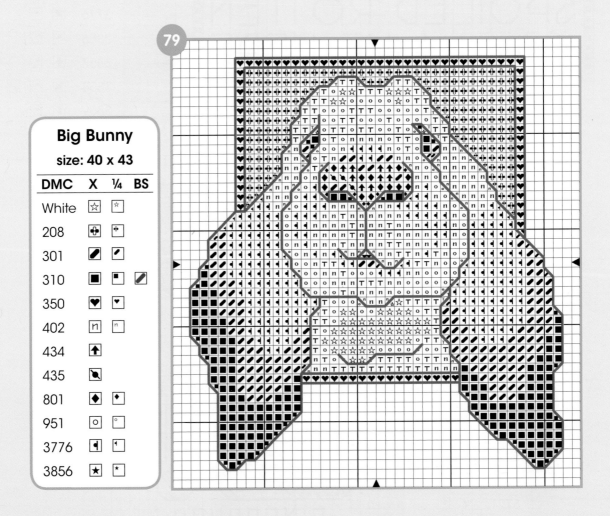

Big Bunny

size: 40 x 43

DMC	X	¼	BS
White	☆	☆	
208	⊕	⊕	
301	╱	╱	
310	■	■	╱
350	♥	♥	
402	n	n	
434	⬆		
435	◧		
801	◆	◆	
951	○	○	
3776	◀	◀	
3856	★	★	

Blue Parakeet

size: 30 x 59

DMC	X	¼	BS
White	☆	☆	
208	♥	♥	
210	H	H	
310	■	■	╱
402	◀	◀	
413	◆	◆	╱
414	⊥	⊥	
415	Z	Z	
745	I	I	
747	a	a	
762	○	○	
964	✚	✚	
996	↑	↑	
3776	╱	╱	
3846	L	L	

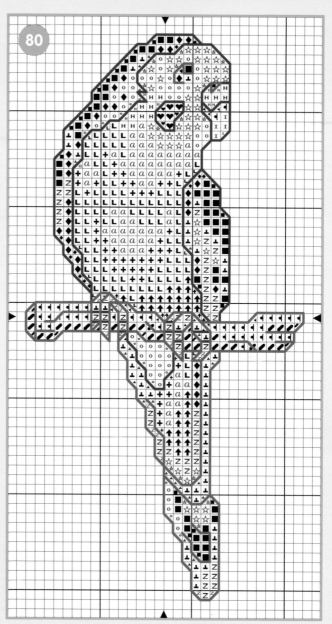

80

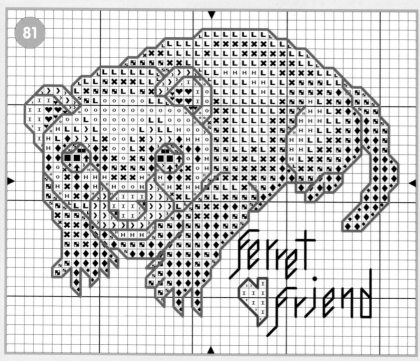

81

Ferret Friend

size: 40 x 32

DMC	X	¼	BS	FK
223	I	I		
310	■	■	╱	
400	↑	↑		
434	■	■		
435	✖	✖		
436	L	L		
738	H	H		
739	○	○		
792			╱	●
801	◆	◆		
3721	♥	♥	╱	
3770	❭	❭		

Box Turtle
size: 38 x 29

DMC	X	¼	BS	FK
301	▨	ᴵ		
310	■	◾	◪	⬤
318	◮	ᴬ		
402	n	ⁿ		
413	◆	◆		
414	◣	◤		
415	H	ᴴ		
792	◖	◗		
793	★	⋆		
909			◪	
913	Z	ᶻ		
3747	❭	˒		
3776	⊙	⊙		
3856	ᴵ	ᴵ		

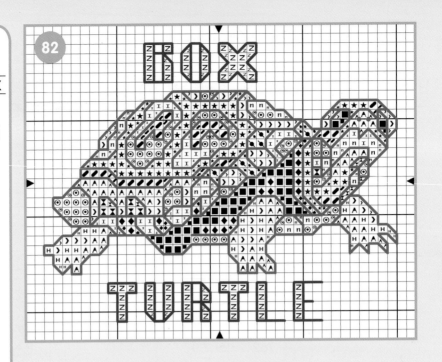

Bunny 1
size: 36 x 50

DMC	X	¼	BS
White	☆	⋆	
151	n	ⁿ	
223	♥	♥	
310	■	◾	◪
400	◆	◆	
413	✖	ˣ	
414	ⓐ	ᵃ	
762	⊠	ˣ	
818	ᴵ	ᴵ	

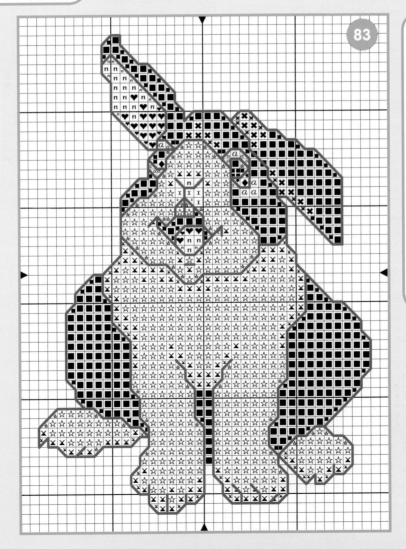

Cheesy Mouse
size: 35 x 38

DMC	X	¼	BS
White		☆	
223	♥	♥	
224	I	I	
310	■	■	╱
400	╱	╱	
413			╱
414	◆	◆	
415	✚	✚	
676	↑	↑	
729	▣	▣	
745	○	○	
762	4	4	
801			╱
3776	◣	◣	

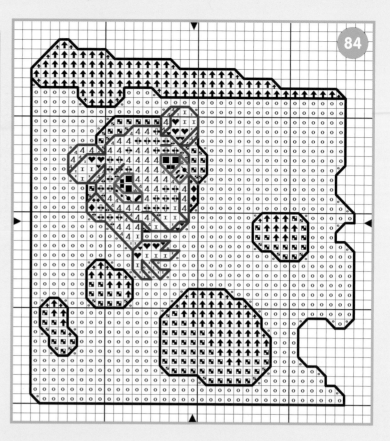

84

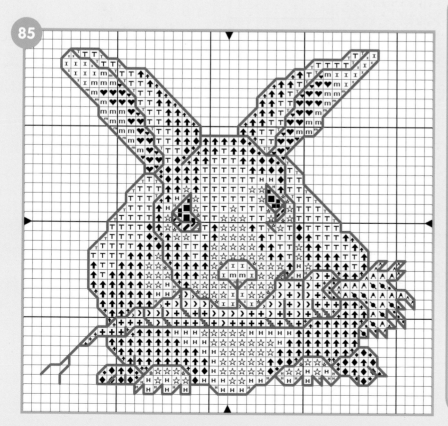

85

Bunny 2
size: 40 x 36

DMC	X	¼	BS
White	☆	☆	
151	m	m	
223	♥	♥	
310	■	■	╱
400	╱	╱	
435	◆	◆	
436	↑	↑	
702	◣	◣	
721	✚	✚	
722	❯	❯	
738	T	T	
762	H	H	
818	I	I	
907	▲	^	

49

Frog

size: 31x 25

DMC	X	¼	BS
White	☆	☆	
310	■	■	╱
472	◖	◖	
702	◆	◆	
742	◪	◪	
743	Z	Z	
762	▣	▣	
907	n	n	
3823	❯	❯	

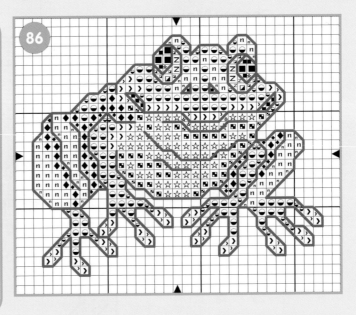

86

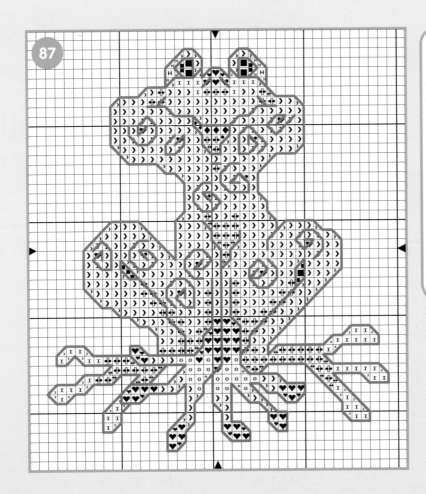

87

Froggie

size: 37 x 42

DMC	X	¼	BS
310	■	■	╱
350	♥	♥	
472	❯	❯	
604	○	○	
722	I	I	
743	H	H	
907	✛	✛	
3345	◆	◆	

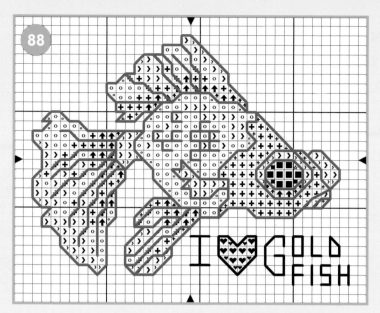

Gold Fish

size: 34 x 26

DMC	X	¼	BS
White	☆		
224	♥	♥	
310	■	▪	╱
742	✚	+	
743	○	°	
744	❯	❯	
781	◆		╱
783	⬆	↑	

Triggerfish

size: 33 x 23

DMC	X	¼	BS	FK
White			╱	●
310	■	▪	╱	
350	♥		╱	
721	✖	⊠		
722	▲	▲		
742	Z	z		
744	○	°		
747	❯	❯		
996	⬆	↑		
3846	I	I		

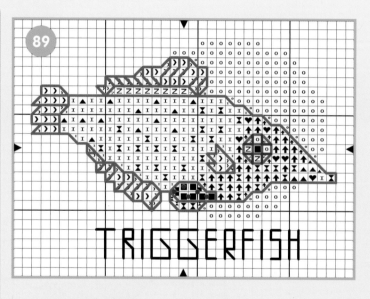

Box Fish

size: 34 x 28

DMC	X	¼	BS
310	■	▪	╱
350	◆	◆	╱
721	◪	◪	
722	T	T	
744	Z	z	
745	○	°	
973	m	m	
3820	◣	◣	
3852	⬆	↑	

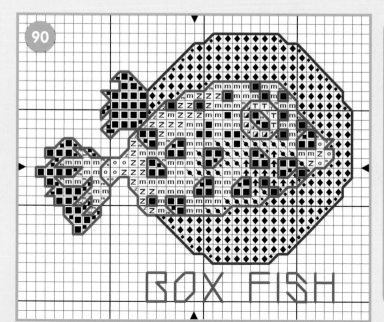

Hamster
size: 39 x 27

DMC	X	¼	BS
White	☆	☆	
151	m	m	
223	▣	▣	
301	◥	◥	
310	■	■	∕
402	✚	✚	
413			∕
415	L	L	
762	H	H	
818	❯	❯	
951	I	I	
3721	♥	♥	
3776	◆	◆	
3856	○	○	

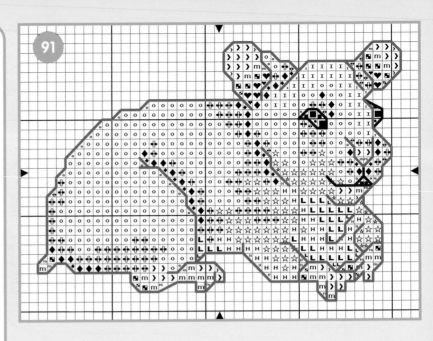

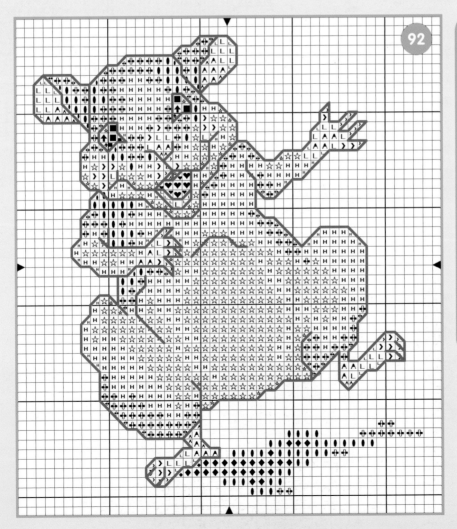

Hamster Dance
size: 42 x 48

DMC	X	¼	BS
White	☆	☆	
151	L	L	
310	■	■	∕
318	◖	◖	
414	◆	◆	
415	✚	✚	
762	H	H	
801	↑	↑	
818	❯	❯	
3721	♥	♥	
3733	A	A	

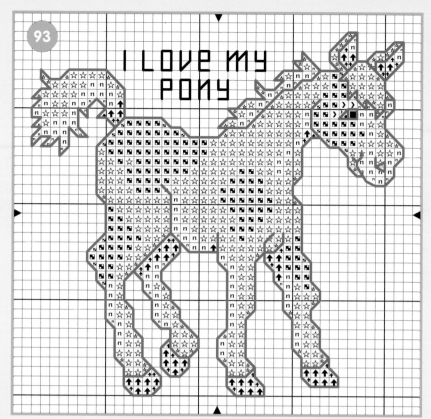

93

I Love my
PONY

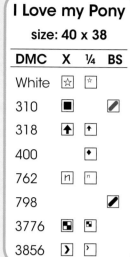

I Love my Pony
size: 40 x 38

DMC	X	¼	BS
White	☆	☆	
310	■		╱
318	⬆	⬆	
400		◆	
762	n	n	
798			╱
3776	◨	◨	
3856	❯	❯	

Love a Bunny
size: 38 x 44

DMC	X	¼	BS
White	☆	☆	
151	Z	z	
223	♥	♥	
310	■	■	╱
318	◣	◤	
400	⊥	⊥	
414	⬆	⬆	
415	◨	◨	
762	I	I	
801	◆	◆	╱
818	❯	❯	
3776	m	m	
3846	✚	✚	

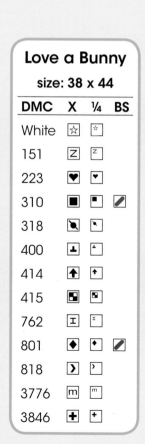

94

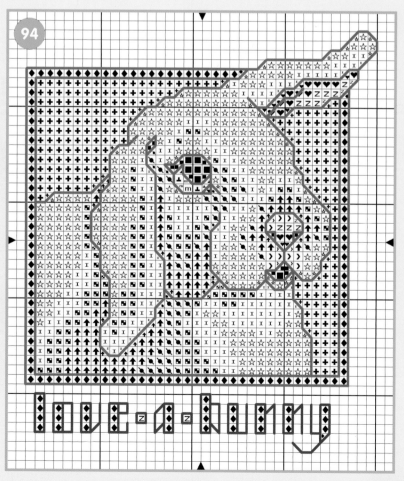

love-a-bunny

53

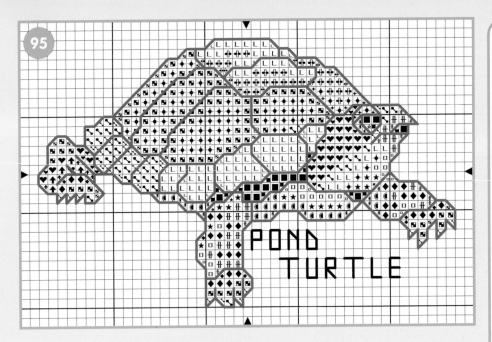

Pond Turtle
size: 45 x 28

DMC	X	¼	BS
White	☆		
310	■	■	
402	★	⁎	╱
414	◆	◆	
504	◥	◥	
563	✦	✦	
745	⊞	⊞	
747	L	L	
964	⊞	⊞	
3776	◖	◖	
3847	⬆	⬆	╱
3848	♥	♥	
3849	◰	◰	
3856	▢	▢	

Lovebirds
size: 43 x 37

DMC	X	¼	BS	FK
White	☆	☆		
310	■	■	╱	●
350	◪	◪		
413	◆	◆		
415	⊞	⊞		
435	⬆	⬆		
436	○	○		
702	△	△		
721	✕	✕		
722	H	H		
744	⟩	⟩		
907	◥	◥		
3345	◿	◿		
3721	♥	♥		
3856	ⲑ			

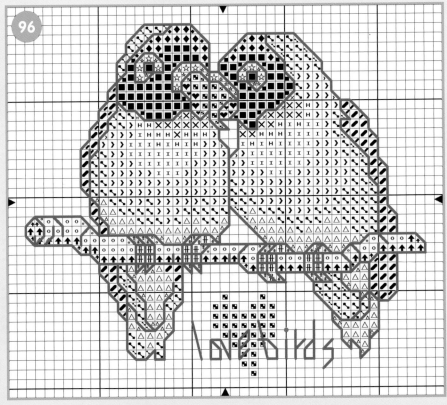

Parrot

size: 40 x 70

DMC	X	¼	BS
310	■	◪	╱
318	▲	◸	
350	n	n	
415	a	a	
702	◪	◪	
721	o	o	
722	T	T	
732	L	L	
734	◣	◥	
743	✚	✚	
744	H		
745	⟩	⟩	
792	⬆	⬆	
809	Z	z	
816	♥	♥	
839	◆	◆	
840	▮	▮	
841	m	m	
842	I	I	
907	⊞	⊞	
3776	4	4	

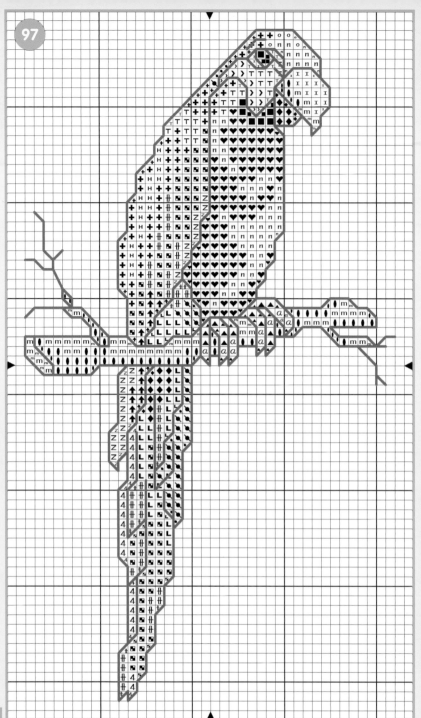

97

98

Beta Fish

size: 31 x 27

DMC	X	¼	BS
208	⬆	⬆	╱
209	✖	✖	
310	■	◪	╱
350	♥	♥	
996	╱	◪	
3842	◆	◆	
3846	★	★	

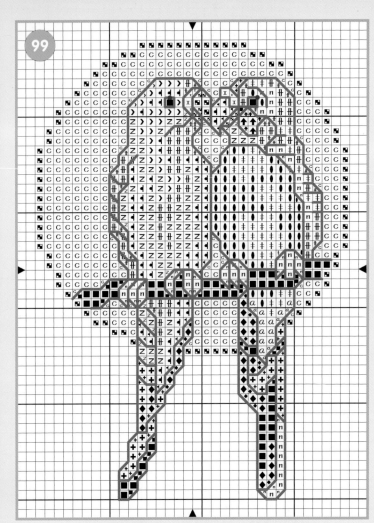

Parakeet Pair

size: 34 x 48

DMC	X	¼	BS	FK
White				●
209	◖	◖		
210	‡	‡		
310	■	■	╱	
318	n	n		
413	◆	◆		
414	✚	✚		
722	◨	◨		
743	Z	z		
744	⊞	⊞		
745	❭	❭		
793	⬆	⬆		
907	C	C		
3747	I	I		
3820	◀	◀		
3846	ⓐ	ⓐ		

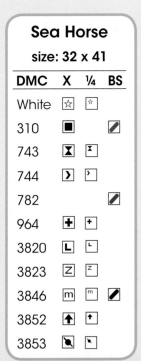

Sea Horse

size: 32 x 41

DMC	X	¼	BS
White	☆	☆	
310	■		╱
743	✖	I	
744	❭	❭	
782			╱
964	✚	✚	
3820	L	L	
3823	Z	z	
3846	m	m	╱
3852	⬆	⬆	
3853	◣	◣	

SEAHORSE